STAR WARS
FOR ACCORDION

T0087025

ISBN 978-1-4950-5999-5

Visit Hal Leonard Online at
www.halleonard.com

Contact us:
Hal Leonard
7777 West Bluemound Road
Milwaukee, WI 53213
Email: info@halleonard.com

In Europe, contact:
Hal Leonard Europe Limited
42 Wigmore Street
Marylebone, London, W1U 2RN
Email: info@halleonardeurope.com

In Australia, contact:
Hal Leonard Australia Pty. Ltd.
4 Lentara Court
Cheltenham, Victoria, 3192 Australia
Email: info@halleonard.com.au

ACROSS THE STARS

(Love Theme from *STAR WARS: ATTACK OF THE CLONES*)

Music by JOHN WILLIAMS

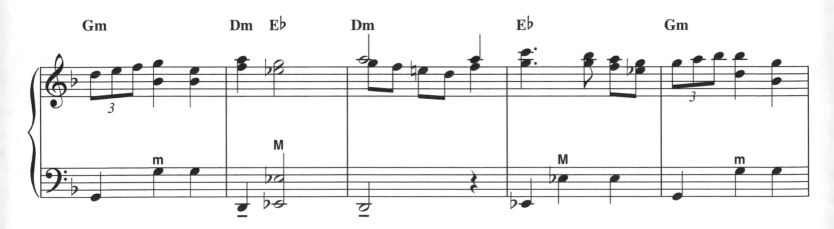

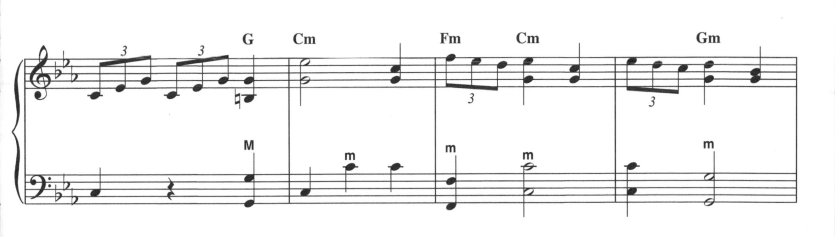

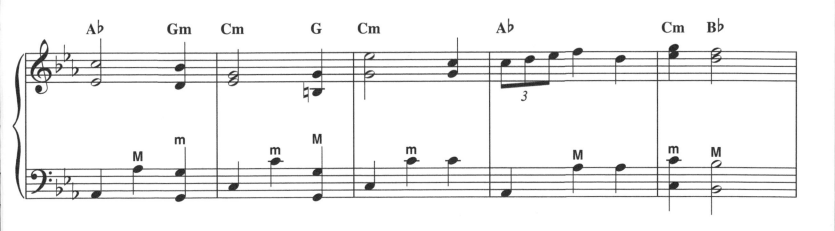

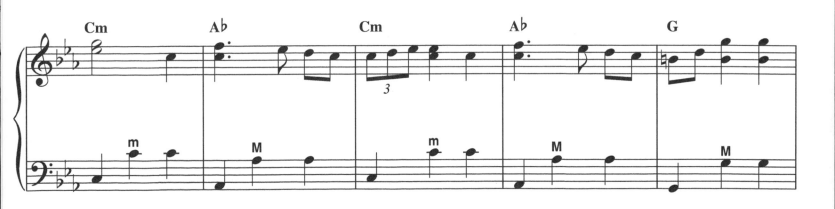

4

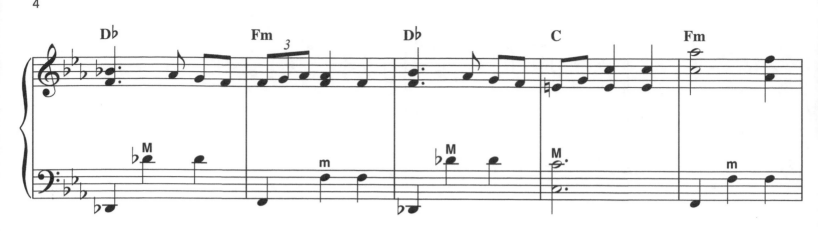

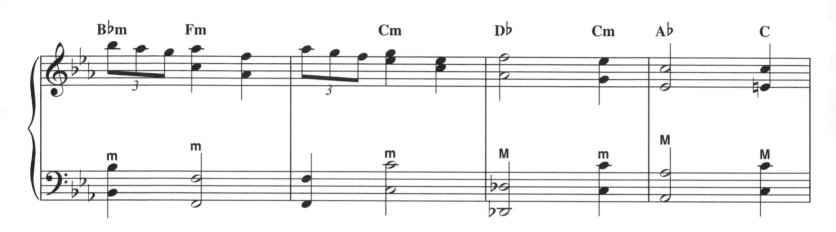

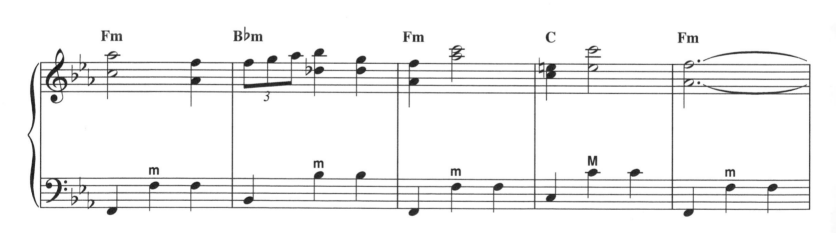

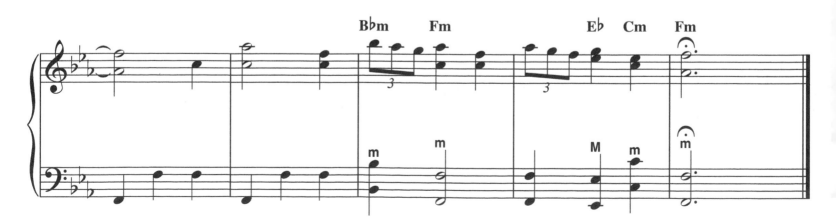

DUEL OF THE FATES
from STAR WARS: THE PHANTOM MENACE

Music by JOHN WILLIAMS

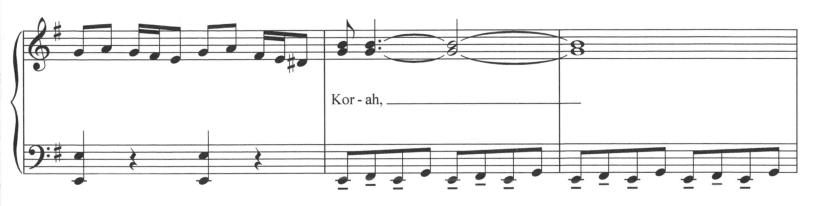

Kor - ah, _____

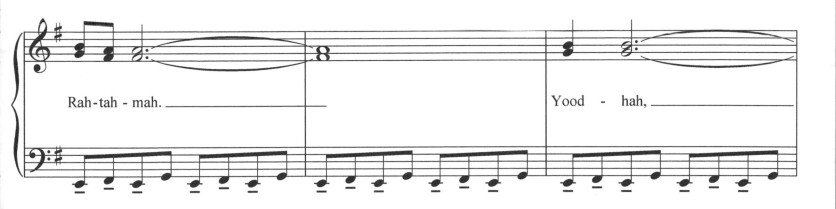

Rah-tah - mah. _____ Yood - hah, _____

Kor - ah. _____

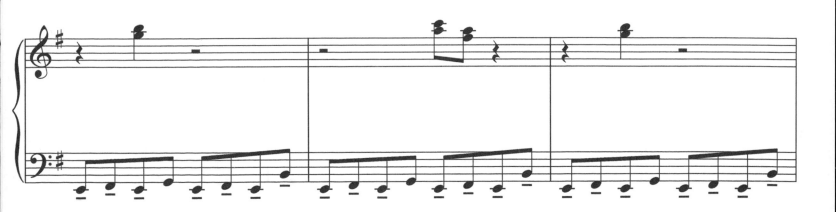

Kor - ah, _____

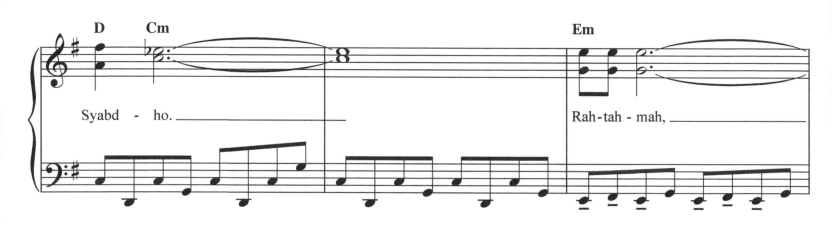

Syabd - ho. _____ Rah-tah - mah, _____

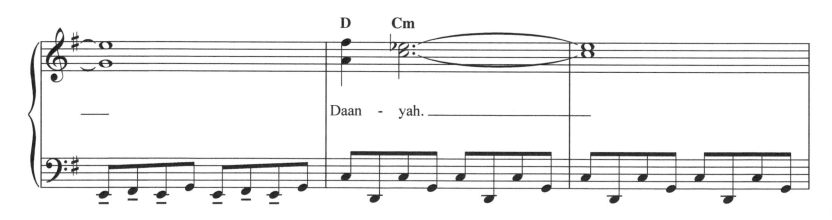

_____ Daan - yah. _____

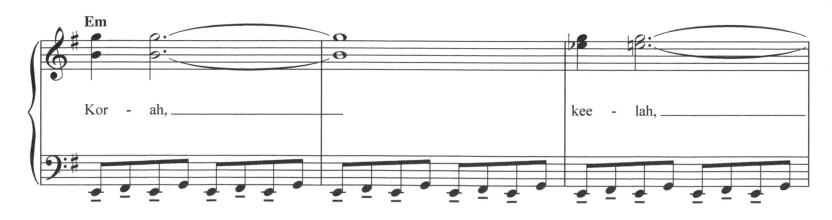

Kor - ah, _____ kee - lah, _____

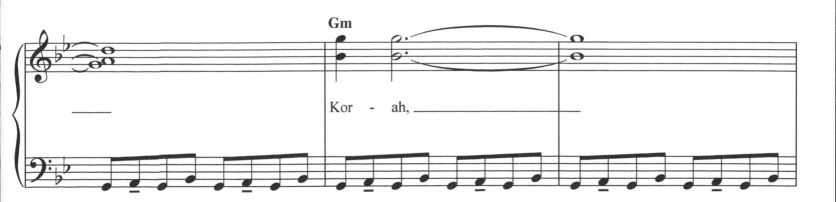

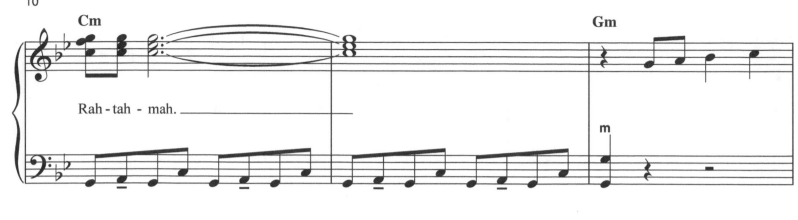

Rah - tah - mah. _____

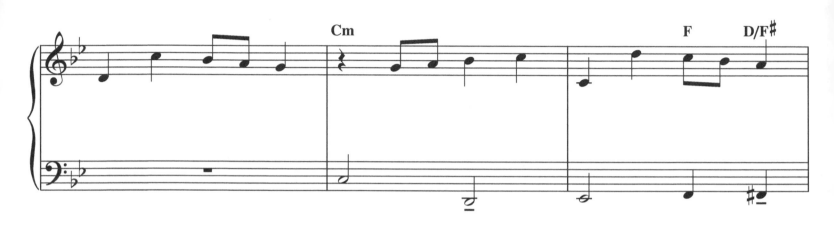

Kor - ah, _____   Daan - yah. _____

Kor - ah, _____

CANTINA BAND
from STAR WARS: A NEW HOPE

Music by JOHN WILLIAMS

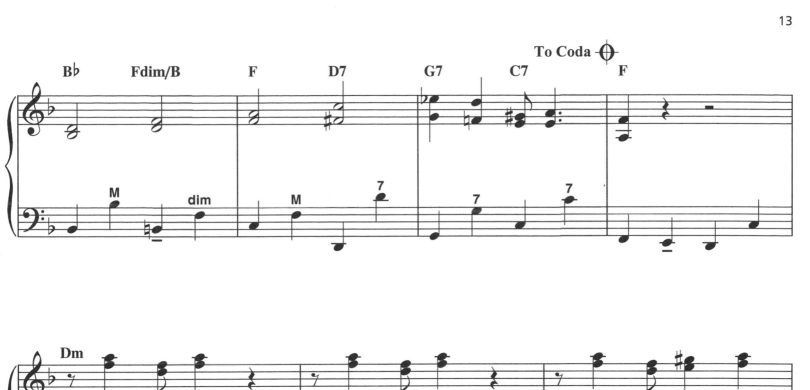

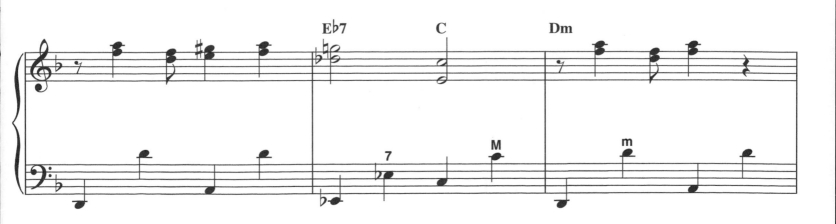

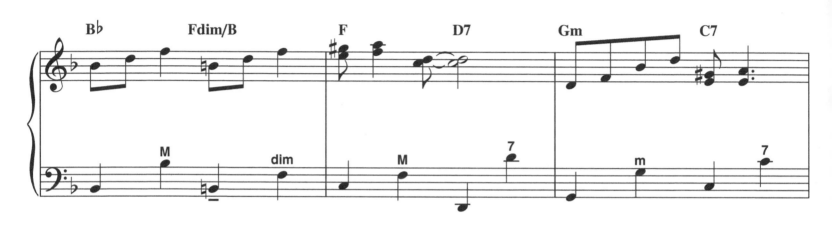

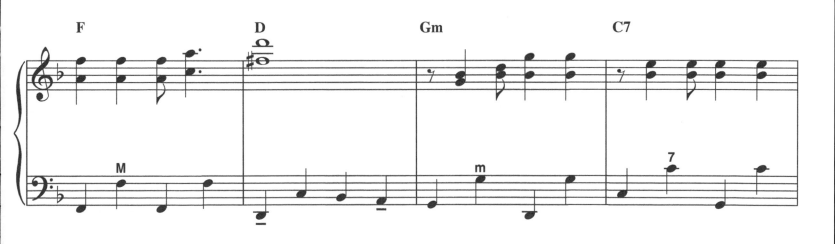
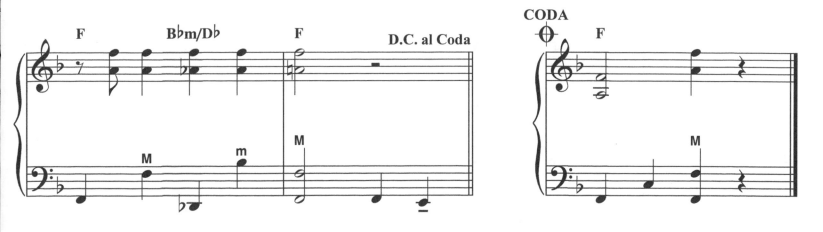

THE IMPERIAL MARCH
(Darth Vader's Theme)
from STAR WARS: THE EMPIRE STRIKES BACK

Music by JOHN WILLIAMS

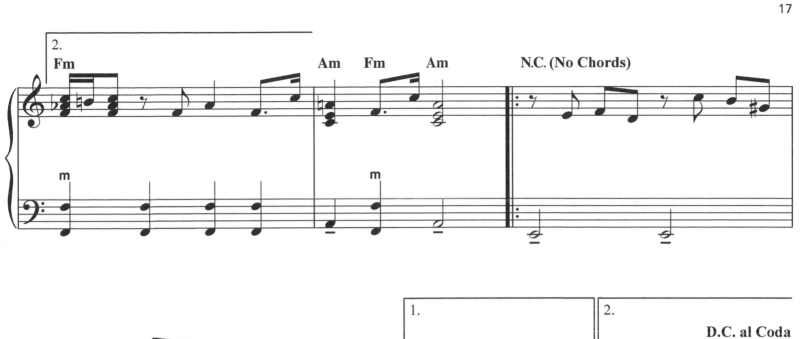

LUKE AND LEIA

from STAR WARS: RETURN OF THE JEDI

Music by JOHN WILLIAMS

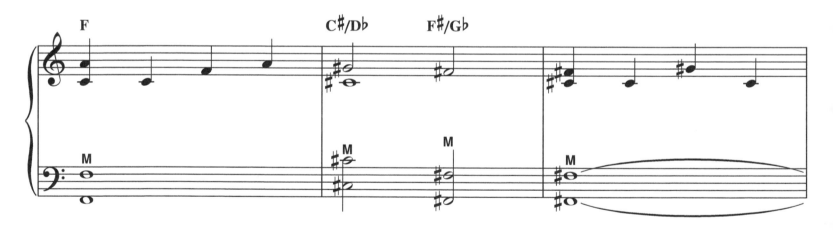

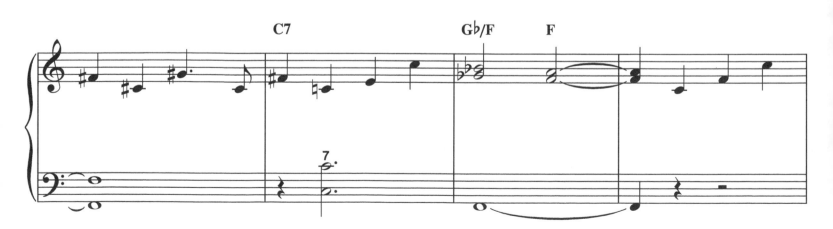

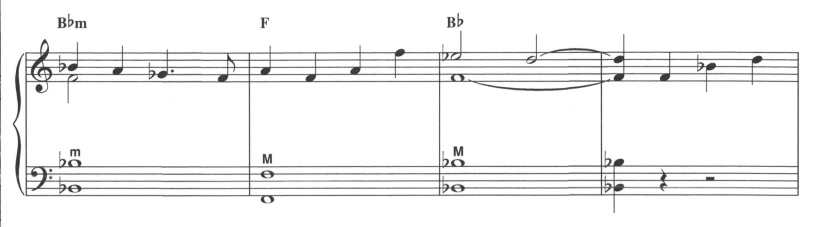

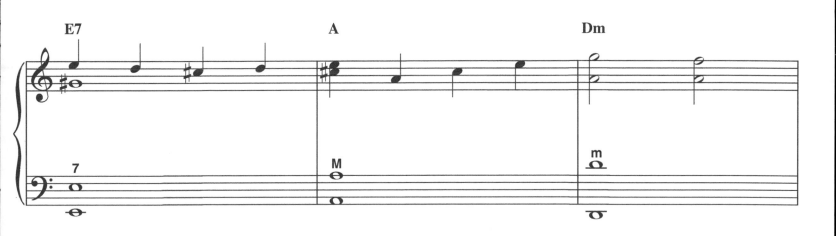

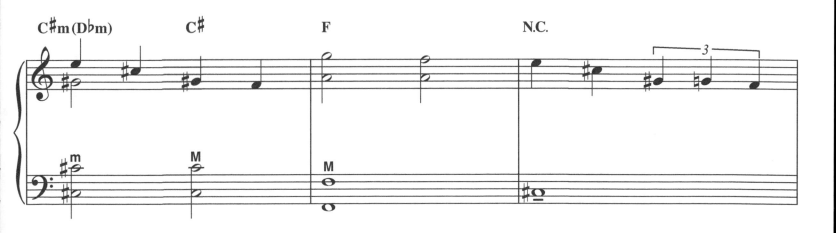

MARCH OF THE RESISTANCE
from STAR WARS: THE FORCE AWAKENS

Music by JOHN WILLIAMS

MAY THE FORCE BE WITH YOU
from STAR WARS: A NEW HOPE

Music by JOHN WILLIAMS

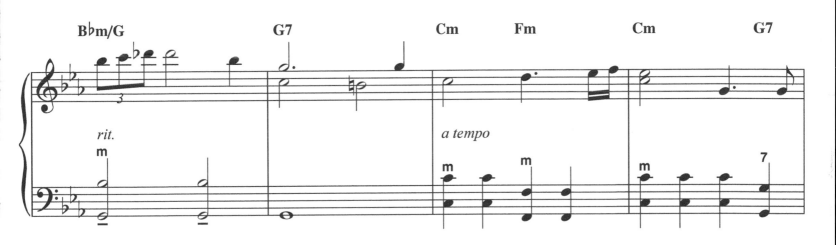

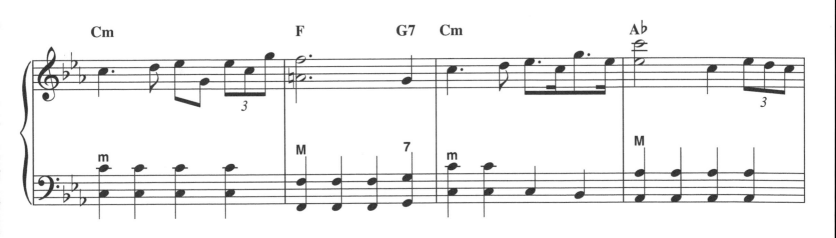

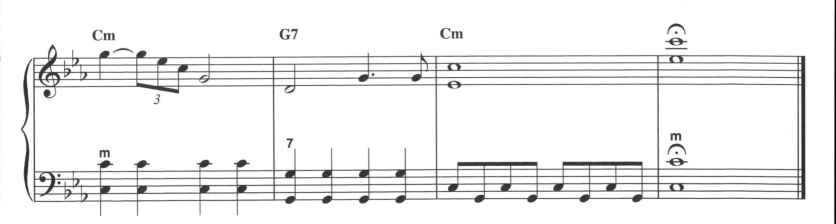

PRINCESS LEIA'S THEME

from STAR WARS: A NEW HOPE

Music by JOHN WILLIAMS

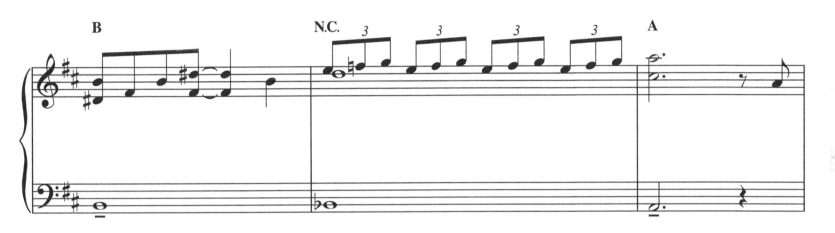

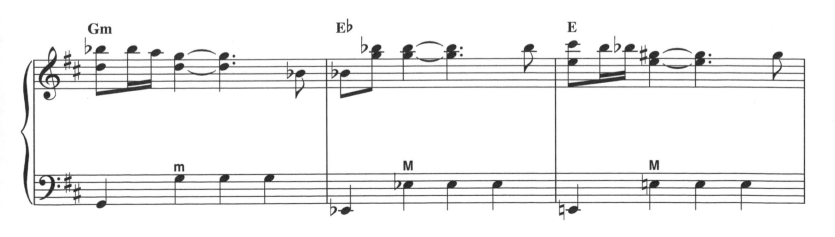

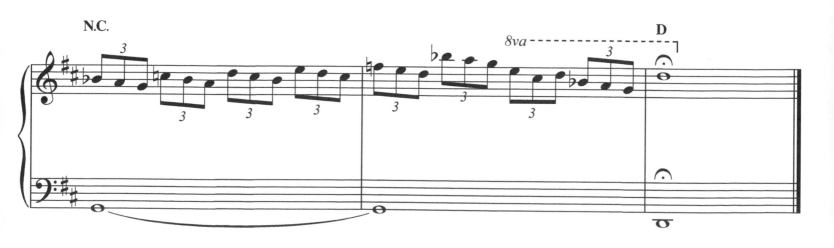

REY'S THEME
from STAR WARS: THE FORCE AWAKENS

Music by JOHN WILLIAMS

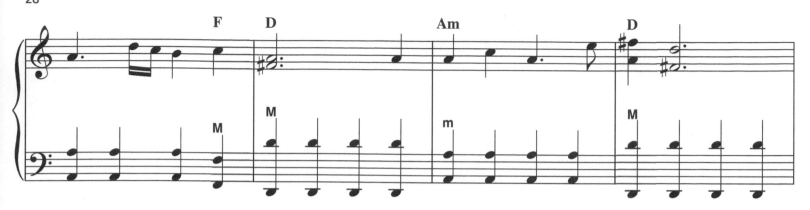

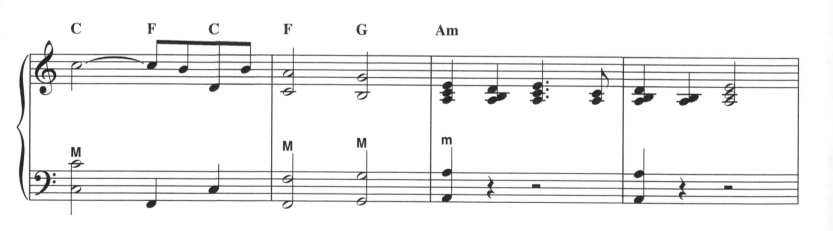

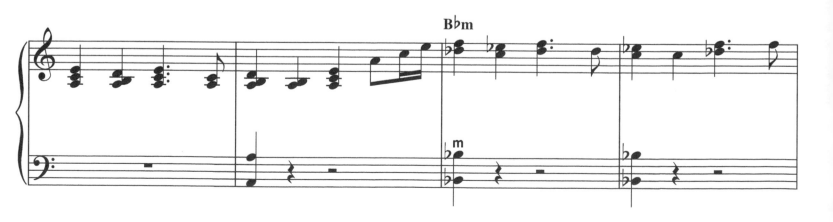

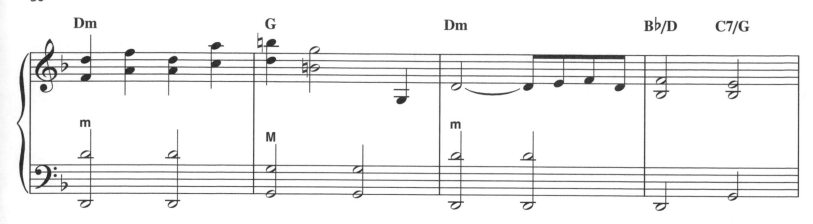

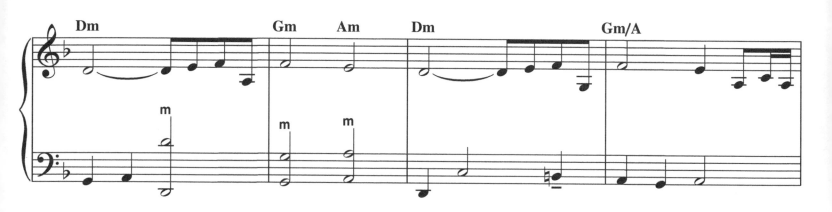

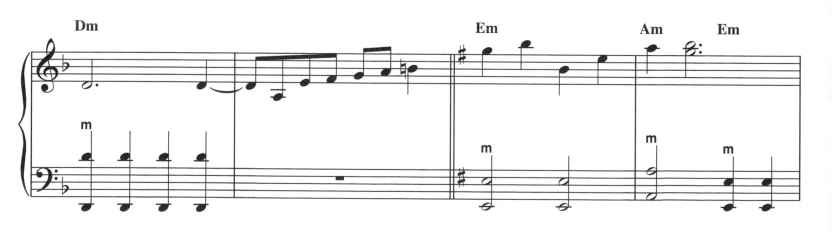

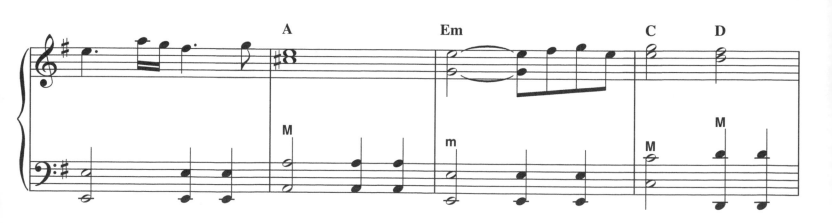

STAR WARS
(Main Theme)
from STAR WARS: A NEW HOPE

Music by JOHN WILLIAMS

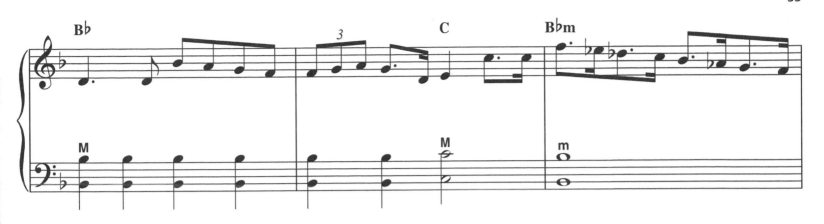

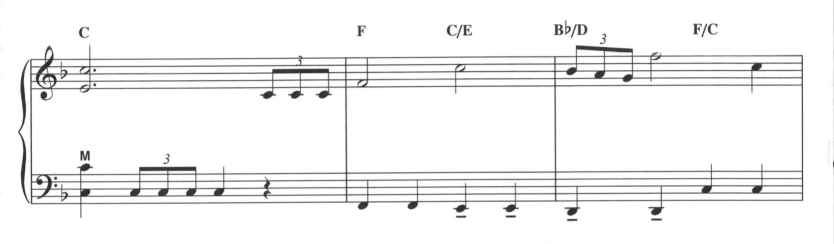

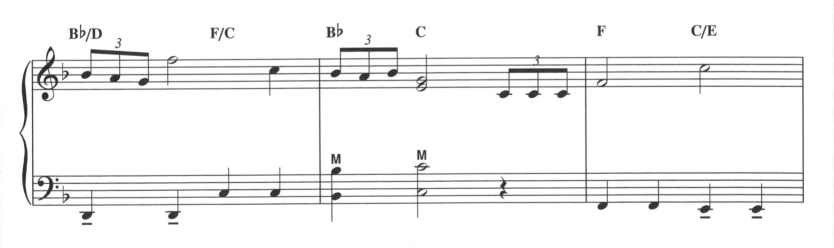

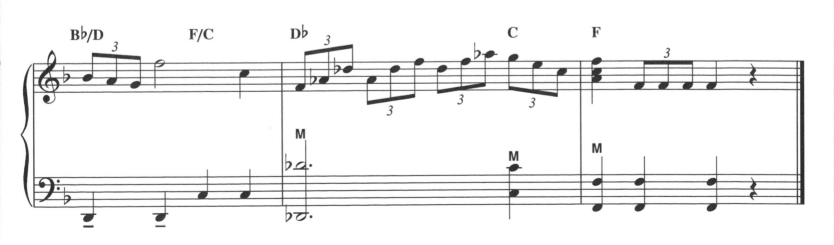

THE THRONE ROOM *and* END TITLE

from STAR WARS: A NEW HOPE

Music by JOHN WILLIAMS

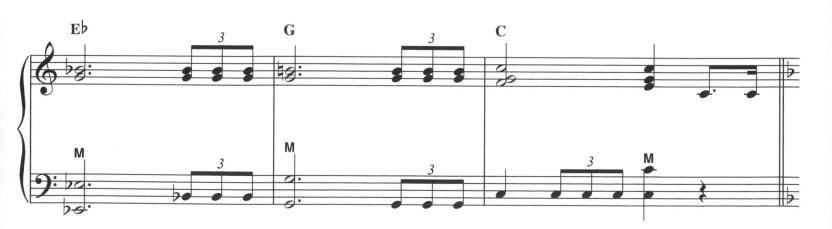

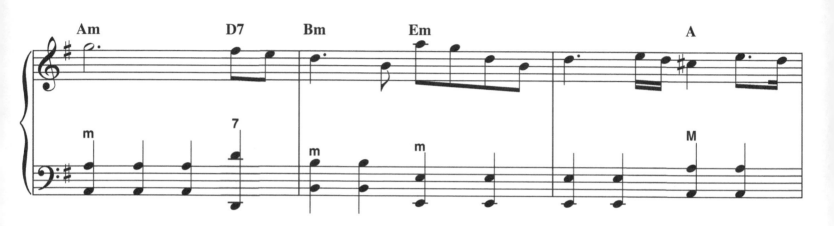

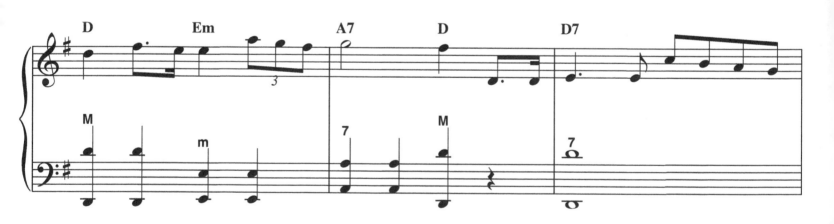

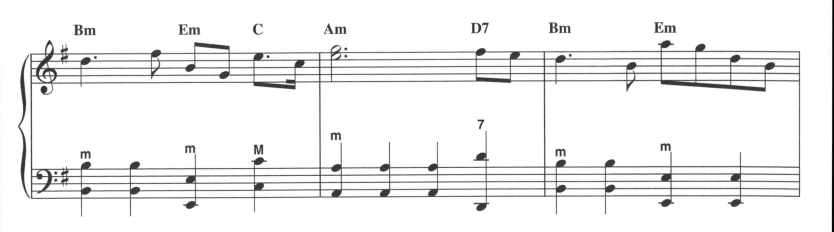

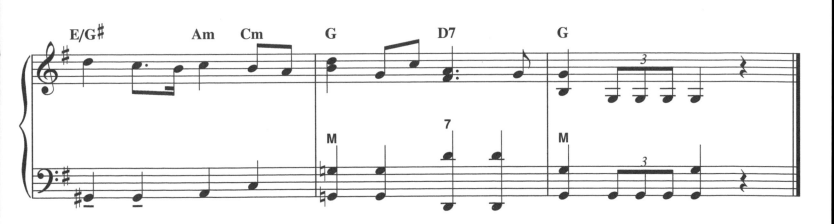

YODA'S THEME
from STAR WARS: THE EMPIRE STRIKES BACK

Music by JOHN WILLIAMS

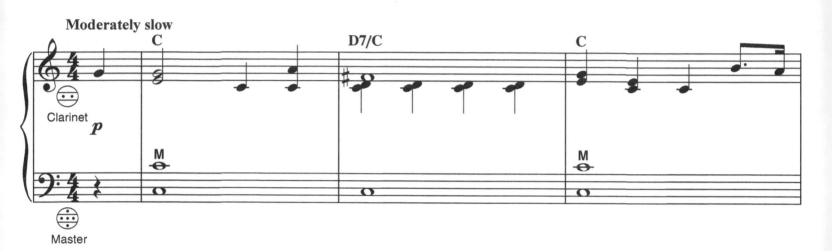

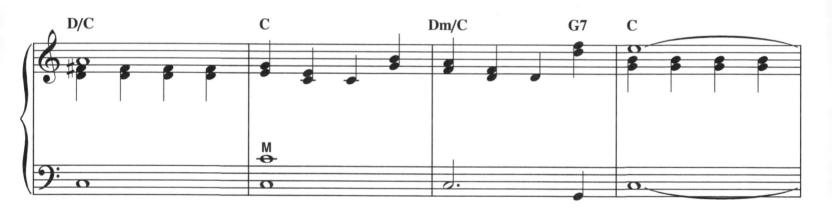

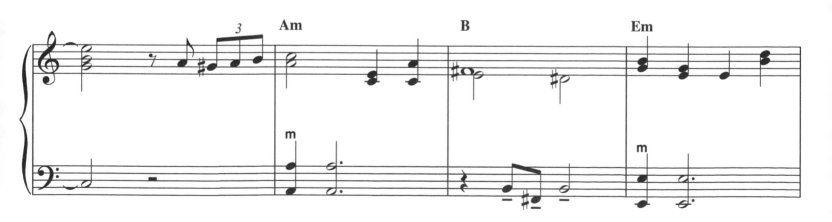

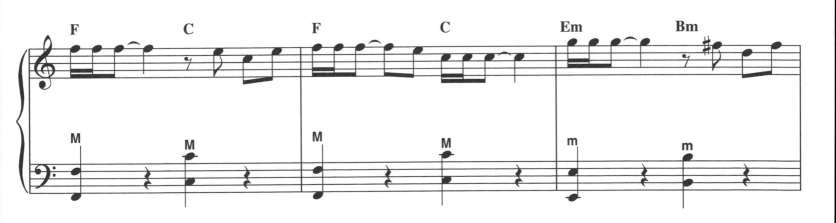

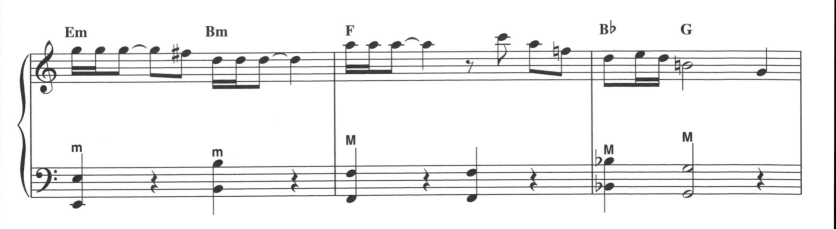

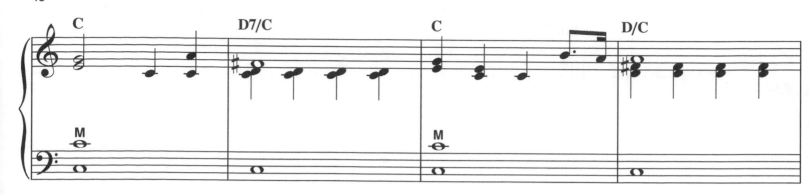

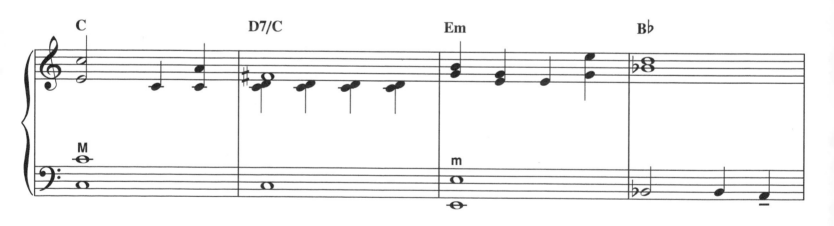

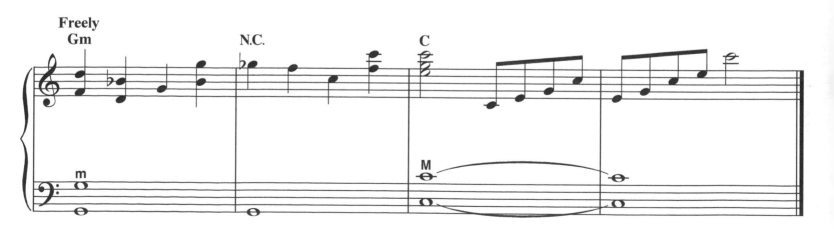